The Lion's Tail and Eyes

The Lion's Tail and Eyes

*Poems written out of laziness
and silence*

by

JAMES WRIGHT, WILLIAM DUFFY,
AND ROBERT BLY

1962

THE SIXTIES PRESS

Acknowledgments are made to the editors of the *San Francisco Review, Poetry, Chicago Choice, The Minnesota Review, The Paris Review,* and *The Sixties*, in which some of these poems have appeared.

Publication of this book was made possible, in part, by grants from Amazon.com; the National Endowment for the Arts, which believes that a great nation deserves great art; and with public funds from the New York State Council on the Arts, a State Agency.

First Edition

ISBN: 978-1-935210-65-8

Printed and bound in the United States of America.

Library of Congress Control Number: 2014947461

White Pine Press
P.O. Box 236
Buffalo, New York 14201
www.whitepine.org

NOTE

THE title, *The Lion's Tail and Eyes,* was suggested by a friend. When Kate Skattebol saw some of the poems in this book, she said that they seemed very strange to her, as if an artist had drawn a lion, but had only drawn in the eyes and the tail. We have to understand that the rest of the lion is there.

One purpose of poetry is to forget about what you know, and think about what you don't know. There is an old idea that only by leaving the body can a man think. Such a leaving concerns the body of knowledge as well as the physical body. After all, as Montale says, if the purpose of poetry lay in making oneself understood, there would be no purpose in writing it.

There are many kinds of poems. The poem that has dominated in the English language for several hundred years is the poem of direct statement. "The proper study of mankind is man." Occasionally this will be mixed with other things. "Time present and time past are both perhaps present in time future."

In 1914, a poetry of pictures emerged. "Petals on a wet black bough." In the *Cantos*, these pictures are mixed with direct statements. This interest in using pictures as a foundation for poetry was misnamed "Imagism." It did not use images. As Yves Bonnefoy says, "An interior sea lighted by turning eagles. This is an image."

The rationalistic statement, which is the foundation of the poetry of direct statement, is good for describing what we have already thought. It ignores the outer world. This is why we have so few clear descriptions of the contemporary life around us in English poetry.

The poetry of pictures is very good for describing the outer world. The poem becomes an extension of the eye, rather than of the brain. This poetry has produced very good work, particularly in Pound and William Carlos Williams.

The fundamental world of poetry, however, is the inward world. The poem expresses what we are just beginning to think, thoughts we have not yet thought. The poem must catch these thoughts alive, holding them in language that is also alive, flexible and animal-like as they.

The poem with images is therefore like a lion about to come into existence. A person meets the poem among trees at night. On the path in front of him, he sees a lion who does not know that he is there. The lion is changing from his old ancient substance back into a visible body. So far the tip of the tail, the ears, the eyes, and perhaps a paw or two have come.

ROBERT BLY.

The Lion's Tail

and Eyes

JAMES WRIGHT

Lying in a Hammock at William Duffy's Farm in Pine Island, Minnesota

Over my head, I see the bronze butterfly,
Asleep on the black trunk,
Blowing like a leaf in green shadow.
Down the ravine behind the empty house,
The cowbells follow one another
Into the distances of the afternoon.
To my right,
In a field of sunlight between two pines,
The droppings of last year's horses
Blaze up into golden stones.
I lean back, as the evening darkens and comes on.
A chicken-hawk floats over, looking for home.
I have wasted my life.

A Dream of Burial

Nothing was left of me
But my right foot
And my left shoulder.
They lay white as the skein of a spider floating
In a field of snow toward a dark building
Tilted and stained by wind.
Inside the dream I dreamed on.

A parade of old women
Sang softly above me,
Faint as mosquitoes near still water.

So I waited, in my corridor.
I listened for the sea
To call me.
I knew that, somewhere outside, the horse
Stood saddled, browsing in grass,
Waiting for me.

In Fear of Harvests

It has happened
Before : nearby,
The nostrils of slow horses
Breathe evenly,
And the brown bees drag their high garlands
Heavily,
Toward hives of snow.

The Undermining of the Defense Economy

Stairway, face, window,
Mottled animals
Running over the public buildings.
Maple and elm.
In the autumn
Of early evening,
A pumpkin
Lies on its side,
Turning yellow as the face
Of a discharged general.
It's no use complaining, the economy
Is going to hell with all these radical
Changes,
Girls the color of butterflies
That can't be sold.
Only after nightfall,
Little boys lie still, awake,
Wondering, wondering,
Delicate little boxes of dust.

Spring Images

Two athletes
Are dancing in the cathedral
Of the wind.

A butterfly lights on the branch
Of your green voice.

Small antelopes
Fall asleep in the ashes
Of the moon.

The Jewel

There is this cave
In the air behind my body
That nobody is going to touch:
A cloister, a silence
Closing around a blossom of fire.
When I stand upright in the wind,
My bones turn to dark emeralds.

As I Step Over a Puddle at the End of Winter,

I Think of an Ancient Chinese Governor

> *And how can I, born in evil days*
> *And fresh from failure, ask a kindness*
> *Of fate?*
> (—written A.D. 819)

Po Chu-i, balding old politician,
What's the use?
I think of you,
Uneasily entering the gorges of the Yang-Tze,
When you were being towed up the rapids
Toward some political job or other
In the city of Chungshou.
You made it, I guess,
By dark.

But it is 1960, it is almost Spring again,
And the tall rocks of Minneapolis
Build me my own black twilight
Of bamboo ropes and waters.
Where is Yuan Chen, the friend you loved?
Where is the sea, that once solved the whole
    loneliness
Of the Midwest?   Where is Minneapolis?   I can see
    nothing
But the great terrible oak tree darkening with winter.
Did you find the city of isolated men beyond
    mountains?
Or have you been holding the end of a frayed rope
For a thousand years?

Milkweed

While I stood here, in the open, lost in myself,
I must have looked a long time
Down the corn-rows, beyond grass,
The small house,
White walls, animals lumbering toward the barn.
I look down now. It is all changed.
Whatever it was I lost, whatever I wept for
Was a wild, gentle thing, the small dark eyes
Loving me in secret.
It is here. At a touch of my hand,
The air fills with delicate creatures
From the other world.

From a Bus Window in Central Ohio, Just Before a Thunder Shower

Cribs loaded with roughage huddle together
Before the north clouds.
The wind tiptoes between poplars.
The silver-maple leaves squint
Toward the ground.
An old farmer, his scarlet face
Apologetic with whiskey, swings back a barn door
And calls a hundred black-and-white Holsteins
From the clover field.

Twilights

The big stones of the cistern behind the barn
Are soaked in whitewash.
My grandmother's face is a small maple leaf
Pressed in a secret box.
Locusts are climbing down into the dark green
    crevices
Of my childhood. Latches click softly in the trees.
    Your hair is gray.

The arbors of the cities are withered.
Far off, the shopping centers empty and darken.

A red shadow of steel mills.

WILLIAM DUFFY

Poem on Forgetting the Body

Riding on the inner side of the blackbird's
Wings, I feel the long
Warm flight to the sea ;
Dark, black in the trees at night.
Along the railroad tracks
In men's minds wild roses grow.
Lingering as ripe black olives
I go down the stairs of the little leaves,
To the floating continent
Where men forget their bodies,
Searching for the tiny
Grain of sand behind their eyes.

How to Begin a Poem

Even in this chair of mine
In my half-darkening library,
I leave it with each vein and capillary,
Slowly yielding to my shadow.

But, suddenly, my airedale jumps
Across the chrysanthemum bed,
A garden of sane fathers,
Botanical, blossomy, yielding in the dusk.

I was looking at something tonight :
A white guitar on a brown arm ;
A courtyard, maybe, full of tulips.

But my flattering daughter of Latin
Opens my porcelain soul
To pray socially, seriously,
In the language of horses.

Elk

Sleeping alone again on my linen pillow, I dream
Of haunting journeys into antelope lands
To dark dens lined with lacy ferns,
Green on grey stones, and vines in my arms.

Again the wild boar of the forest is in me
In all the beds and grassy caves
The long goodbyes, the kiss meetings, glances,

Sleeping alone now in the windy limbs of my linden
    trees
I see the cardinal's nest, red clover fields,
Governors, princes, islands of silver mines:

Still . . . no sound . . . but the bleaking grey birds;
You are in the mists of my orange mornings,
And when you pull my hand, I am the elk
Standing . . . sleeping . . . in your darkening forest.

Poem

Crying in your bed at night, —
The wild geese comfort you.

They bring you to wild rice fields and mown hay,
Not to the golden leaves of money,

To old asylums, sugar drinks,
Maids towering on tombstone cliffs ;

They leave your eyes looking like pear-seeds,
Your body feeling like legs and twine,

And your throat with the taste of old wine
Behind the walls of Carcassonne.

Slowly

Slow afternoons — to dusk,
Winter's early night, dark dusk of
Loneliness . . .

One dreams of highwaymen.

Premonitions

The wild piercing railroad
Whistle at dawn,
A mad dog's groaning howl
Comes to us from bowels
Of old volcanoes.

The cold sweat of
Loggers on hard winter mornings,
The scent that makes the coonhound
Bay miles from his fight,
Premonitions of our death,

Brought to us sometimes in dreams,
In moonings, quick sudden starts,
Friends living in us whom
We've never met.

The Horse is Loose

Outside, below my window
The big bay horse is loose
Twisting the dry snow-grass on his yellow teeth.
It is trying to snow . . .
And his brown ears are waiting.

A king stands poised, waiting, in an old
Armenian hat, on a rusty ship
Two thousand miles from any
Atlas.

You talked to me last night of blueberries
And warm raisin drinks and songs . . .
Of hands of servants bathing someone
In the still inlets of the Mediterranean.

But below my window the ground is hard.
This patch of field has only Indian memories.
And I am waiting alone for that tiny sound
Which brings cold terror to hounds
And the sudden jerks in a sleeping man.

Marsh Nest

Backing behind the wooden pale
Of my ancestors and singing a lifting
Song of some lost marsh's nest,

In a lonely wood where only
One flower has its choice to live,
I'll send an angel plucking a lyre.

Darkness may come on a summer noon,
But when the sun and moon are mortal
It gives a man time to clean his glasses.

Take your old hat and wave at me.

Rendering

Before that silver whistle blew
I was a stony green island, a foggy thought,
Foamy waves breaking a boat's stern,
Listless, in a kitchen boiling potatoes.

Now I hear buried notes through stones,
That crack my bony temples, burst my vessels,
Echoing in the shells and the deep sea caves.

This Lion of Loneliness

Alone in the dark garden now
Where I have bathed myself in its
Inky waters, a pistol points at me.

I think of the stale parchment kisses of law,
The lives and losses of men at sea,
And the lonely bed of a dying nun.

This lion of loneliness and love snarls
Less as he gnaws the souls of men
Who lie in the vats, like leather rings.

ROBERT BLY

Silence

The fall has come, clear as the eyes of chickens.
Strange muffled sounds come from the sea,
Sounds of muffled oarlocks,
And swampings in lonely bays,
Surf crashing on unchristened shores,
And the wash of tiny snail shells in the wandering
    gravel.

My body also wanders among these doorposts and
    cars,
Cradling a pen, or walking down a stair
Holding a cup in my hand,
And not breaking into the pastures that lie in the
    sunlight.
This is the sloth of the man inside the body,
The sloth of the body lost among the wandering
    stones of kindness.

Something homeless is looking on the long roads —
A dog lost since midnight, a small duck
Among the odorous reeds,
Or a tiny box-elder bug searching for the window
    pane.
Even the young sunlight is lost on the window pane,
Moving at night like a diver among the bare branches
    silently lying on the floor.

Snowfall in The Afternoon

I

The grass is half-covered with snow.
It was the sort of snowfall that starts in late after-
noon,
And now the little houses of the grass are growing
dark.

II

If I reached my hands down, near the earth,
I could take handfuls of darkness!
A darkness was always there, which we never
noticed.

III

As the snow grows heavier, the cornstalks fade
farther away,
And the barn moves nearer to the house.
The barn moves all alone in the growing storm.

IV

The barn is full of corn, and moving toward us now
Like a hulk blown toward us in a storm at sea;
All the sailors on deck have been blind for many
years.

Late at Night During a Visit of Friends

I

We spent all day fishing and talking.
At last, late at night, I sit at my desk alone,
And rise and walk out in the summery night.
A dark thing hopped near me in the grass.

II

The trees were breathing, the windmill slowly
    pumped.
Overhead the rain clouds that rained on Ortonville
Covered half the stars.
The air was still cool from their rain.

III

It is very late.
I am the only one awake.
Men and women I love are sleeping nearby.

IV

The human face shines as it speaks of things
Near itself, thoughts full of dreams.
The human face shines like a dark sky
As it speaks of those things that oppress the living.

Reading the Translations of William Hung

I am doing nothing, so I read old poems.

It is early spring. Strangely twisted leaves emerge
from their buds.

Tu Fu's spirit enters into the bones of old men
leaving for battle.

Walking around, I feel joy as I see old boards
scattered on the new grass.

Poem in Three Parts

I

Oh, on an early morning I think I shall live forever!
I am wrapped in my joyful flesh,
As the grass is wrapped in its clouds of green.

II

Rising from a bed, where I dreamt
Of long rides past castles and hot coals,
The sun lies happily on my knees ;
I have suffered and survived the night,
Bathed in dark water, like any blade of grass.

III

The strong leaves of the box-elder tree,
Plunging in the wind, call us to disappear
Into the wilds of the universe,
Where we shall sit at the foot of a plant,
And live forever, like the dust.

" Taking The Hands "

Taking the hands of someone you love,
You see they are delicate cages . . .
Tiny birds are singing
In the secluded prairies
And in the deep valleys of the hand.

The Grass-Headed Lion

The smoky morning has come.

The night is over.

The grass-headed lion has gone back to his den.

The ship has sailed over the horizon,

The red wheat pours out,

The rowers are lifting their hats in the morning heat.

The river flows past roots and old wharfs.

Silk waits in attics.

The small snails come out to greet the sun.

Traveller Leaves Appomatox

Nothing can be done, until the pirates hoist their
    black flags,
And the mole, sleeping, rises crowned with leaves,
The wild milk foams on shipboard,
And the masts group in a vast and sleeping harbor.
Boars are tearing at the roots of trees
In Tennessee,
Where the long shrouds of the leaves cover the
    bones of men,
And muskets cry out in the steaming woods all
    night,
And hollow trees, and rotted stumps, and buckles
    cry out !

Dirty papers cover the streets of Harlem ;
I see the half-painted signs,
The anguish,
The conviction that tomorrow will be like today,
That birds must be in cages,
The certainty that the fish is thirsty —
In New York the cables lie all night
Breathing at the sides of streets,

Ready to be placed in concrete ;

Leaving Appomatox, Traveller is moving

Through the stumpy fields, among mosquitoes in the
shape of men ;

We are in pain ;

It is the old pain —

I hear Hoover crying in his sleep,

And sooty trees kneel in Spanish churches, lighting
the candles with their branches.

Dark earth, thirty-five feet deep,

Flows beneath the trees.

Dark flowers floating on the underground lakes.

Ground water is slowly drifting through the honey-
combs of shale;

This water is our water,

It is a new water, pure through many poisoned
stones.

Sparks Of The Body

Yes, I am the son, new born in the Lutheran wastes of Minnesota, like an eye! Writhing on the ground, newly woken from sleep, like a slave who hates the sparks in the body! Woken at winter dark to row in the frozen ocean air, or to scrub the closets in a castle made of black sticks —

Is the body prowling on the shore of the grave ?— like a heap of stones resentful it is not a wing. Where are the friends who are not with us? Heavy smoke of sleep rolls from the body. How long before it begins to burn? And She? Is She in the same anguish?

Evolution From The Fish

This grandchild of fishes
Holds in him a hundred thousand tiny stones.
This nephew of snails, naked
On a bed with a smiling woman, blazing
Under marble roofs, moves toward his own life
Like fur walking. He is fur, mammoth fur growing
As the leaves fall, or slim Indian hands living
Their play of disturbed snakes, heartless life
Passing each other, fur that climbs a wall,
Kissing a woman's skin, leaning against a pillar,
He moves toward the animal, the animal with furry
    head !

What a joy to smell the flesh of a new child !
Like new grass, and the long man with the student
    girl,
Coffee, pale waists, the spirit moving around them,
Moves, dragging a great tail, into the darkness.
And ourselves, blazing up, drawing spiny fish
As we sleep, we throw off the white stones !
The sea serpent ascends with spiral motions,
The man closes a door, sluggish thought enters the
    diamond
To sleep. O do not stop me now ! Let me raise
My hands, fire passes through the soles of my feet—
I am curving back into the mammoth pool !